Egypt

Egypt is one of the countries of northern Africa and covers an area of 1 million square kilometers (400,000 square miles). The early Egyptians settled in the Nile Valley where the soil favored the growth of their crops. These small settlements along the river grew into one of the greatest civilizations the world has ever known, the remains of which can still be seen today.

Agriculture is still the main source of income for most Egyptians, but they no longer have to rely on the annual flooding of the Nile for the fertilization and irrigation of the soil. The Aswan High Dam, completed in 1971, stores water and regulates the flow of the Nile River so that a constant water supply is available. Projects such as this and the discovery of large oilfields are helping Egypt to develop once again, and the Egyptian people can look to a prosperous economy in the future.

In *We Live in Egypt* a cross section of the Egyptian people tell you what their life is like – life in the city, life on the farm, life at school.

Preben Kristensen is a widely traveled photographer, and Fiona Cameron is a freelance writer.

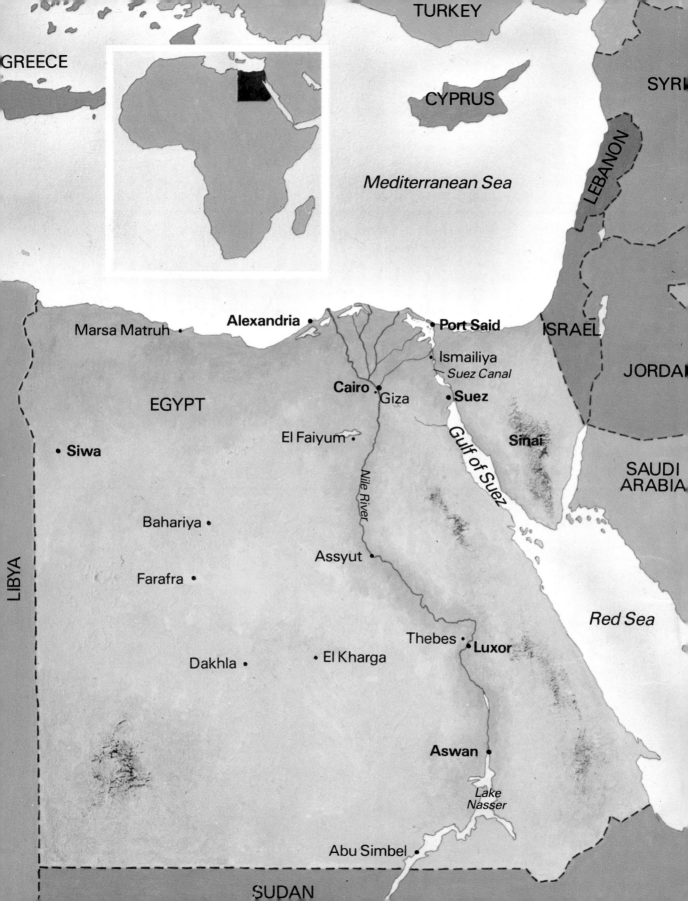

we live in
EGYPT

**Preben Kristensen
and Fiona Cameron**

The Bookwright Press
New York· 1987

Living Here

We live in Argentina
We live in Australia
We live in Belgium and Luxembourg
We live in Brazil
We live in Britain
We live in Canada
We live in the Caribbean
We live in Chile
We live in China
We live in Denmark
We live in East Germany
We live in Egypt
We live in France
We live in Greece
We live in Hong Kong
We live in India
We live in Indonesia
We live in Ireland
We live in Israel

We live in Italy
We live in Japan
We live in Kenya
We live in Malaysia and Singapore
We live in Mexico
We live in the Netherlands
We live in New Zealand
We live in Pakistan
We live in the Philippines
We live in Poland
We live in Portugal
We live in Saudi Arabia
We live in South Africa
We live in Spain
We live in Sweden
We live in the U.S.A.
We live in the Asian U.S.S.R.
We live in the European U.S.S.R.
We live in West Germany

First published in the
United States in 1987 by
The Bookwright Press
387 Park Avenue South
New York, NY 10016

First published in 1986 by
Wayland (Publishers) Ltd
61 Western Road, Hove
East Sussex BN3 1JD, England

© Copyright 1986 Wayland (Publishers) Ltd

ISBN: 0–531–18087–5
Library of Congress Catalog Card Number: 86–70994

Phototypeset by Kalligraphics Ltd
Redhill, Surrey
Printed in Italy by G. Canale & C.S.p.A., Turin

Contents

Joseph Abdel Al Abullbw, *camel dealer*   6

Abdou Ahmed Abdou, *geologist*   8

Dr. Hassan Ragab, *papyrus expert*   10

Tarek Amin, *scuba diving instructor*   12

Wafaa Saad Khamis, *cotton quality controller*   14

Ahmed Hassanain, *civil engineer*   16

Nagwa Fouad, *belly dancer*   18

Dr. Abdul Wadood Shalaby, *Islamic leader*   20

Om Aolooum, *midwife*   22

Osman Ehsan, *cruise ship pilot*   24

Mohamed Khalil, *factory foreman*   26

Bassma Mohamed Aly El Sabae, *schoolgirl*   28

Abdel Kader, *farmer*   30

Mohamed Gaber El Seid, *fisherman*   32

Shahira Mehrez, *craftswoman*   34

Abdul El Hakeem, *soldier*   36

Mohammad El Zayd Ahmet, *felucca captain*   38

Aida Hassan Hamed, *food packager*   40

Soleman Eid Soleman, *Bedouin tribesman*   42

Fatma Shorbagy, *carpet weaver*   44

Mohamed Nasr, *Egyptologist*   46

Badia Osman Soliman, *hotel owner*   48

Mustafa Mohammad Hamama, *shopkeeper*   50

Mrs. Ragabia-Bastawy, *Nubian housewife*   52

Fathi Ahmed Abdel Nabi, *cruise ship captain*   54

Dr. Mamdouh El Beltagui, *Chairman of the State Information Service*   56

Facts   58

Glossary   59

Index   60

"Camels all have different characters"

Joseph Abdel Al Abullbw, 45, has been a camel dealer in the Cairo camel market for the last thirty years. He lives with his wife and children in a wealthy suburb of Cairo.

You can only get into this business if you are born into it. Both my father and grandfather were camel dealers, so camel dealing is in my blood! I was born in Aswan, but moved to Cairo when I was very young. I started helping my father part-time after school when I was eight years old, but became a full-time dealer when I was fifteen.

The camels are all bred in the Sudan, where there is more land available for grazing. They are brought down here by Sudanese traders. First they have to walk from the Sudan to Aswan – this takes them about forty days. Then they are brought down to Cairo by train. Camels can go for two months without water, but even they don't make this journey in the three hottest months of summer. Although there is a small market in Aswan and another one in Cairo, this one at Imbaba is the largest camel market in Egypt and the Sudan.

Camels are proud animals and all have different characters. Most are nervous

Camels carry heavy loads.

6

and must be tied up. But if you lock them up for long, they can get very angry and became dangerous. Once I even had to shoot one. A camel can kill.

The cost of a camel depends on a lot of things and ranges from E£200–700 (equivalent to $150–$500) for a good one. It must be fat and look good, with a large hump and small, even teeth. A large camel may weigh about 450 kg (990 lb). Of course you must be able to recognize any defects or diseases, but that comes with experience. I can recognize a good camel immediately.

I sell camels to three different groups of people: butchers, farmers and middlemen, who will then fatten the camels and resell them to the butchers. The farmers use camels to carry crops because they are very strong. In the south, they are used to carry huge loads of sugarcane.

Joseph can tell how good a camel is just by looking at it.

Every dealer has a mark. Mine is the number 85, painted in Arabic on the right side of the neck. Everyone then knows where a particular camel has come from. I work here every day except Sunday, from early morning until about four in the afternoon. It's my life; I have no hobbies.

I married my cousin, who is also from a camel-dealing family. I have four sons and a daughter. The oldest son is about to graduate from college and will come and work here after his military service. The others are still in college but will also work here eventually. A good education will make them better dealers. I had to leave school early but my brother graduated as a lawyer before he started working here.

People think that a camel dealer should live in a tent in the desert and ride a camel. But that's nonsense. I live in a villa with a large garden in Mohandisin, one of the richest suburbs of Cairo. I'm a rich man and I'm satisfied with my life here.

"Oil drilling is always a gamble"

Thirty-four-year-old Abdou Ahmed Abdou has worked for eight years at the Egyptian Petroleum Research Institute. He is a geologist specializing in chemical analysis of rocks and sediments in the Nile Delta.

Oil is the primary source of energy in Egypt. However, it wasn't discovered here until 1968. Today, Egypt produces about 42 million tons a year, but that figure is expected to grow significantly in the coming years due to promising new finds. This means that oil products are much cheaper here than in Western Europe. However, we also export a good deal of oil which gives us valuable foreign currency. In 1984 we exported oil worth just under $3000 million!

The most important oilfields in Egypt are situated in the Suez Gulf (offshore), the Western Desert and Sinai. The most promising of these are considered to be in the Suez Gulf area and the Western Desert. In the Western Desert alone we have estimated the reserves to be approximately 15,000 million tons.

I study samples of rocks and other sediments to determine the probability of

Many promising oilfields have been discovered in Egypt over the last few years.

8

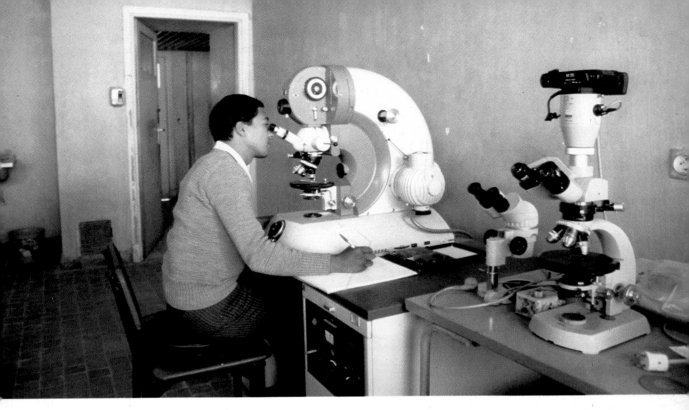

finding oil. We never know with certainty if there is any, so drilling is always a big gamble. However, the sophisticated methods and equipment that we use nowadays make it a lot easier to make a qualified guess.

We begin our search for oil by studying detailed maps and satellite photos looking for certain geological formations. The next step is to examine the geomagnetism and gravity at the site. If this looks promising then we carry out a seismic analysis. The principle is really quite simple: we make an explosion and measure the timing and the pattern of the shock waves as they are reflected from the different layers underground. This provides us with a detailed "map" of the various underground layers, which can extend to a depth of 5 km (3 miles).

We are especially interested in finding layers of clay or other sediments that are particularly rich in organic materials. It is these organic materials which

Abdou studies some rock samples under a microscope.

become oil after being exposed to enormous pressures and temperatures for hundreds of thousands of years. The oil slowly seeps away until it gathers in a fold of porous sandstone surrounded by a layer of confining material like clay or solid rock, which will trap the oil. We have to locate these "pockets" and decide exactly where to drill, which is when the really costly process begins.

The oil industry in Egypt, as in most other countries, is made up of both state-owned and private companies. The enormous investments which are necessary in the exploration for oil have been shared between the Egyptian State and a number of foreign investors. Many people are involved in the process of finding oil and I am only a single cog in a big machine, but it is a fascinating and challenging job.

"Papyrus pushed me into business"

Dr. Hassan Ragab, 75, has spent the last twenty years trying to rekindle people's interest in the everyday life of the ancient Egyptians, by establishing first a Papyrus Institute and then a typical pharaonic village in Cairo.

I've done many interesting things in my life. I started as an engineer, spent time in the army and then went into the diplomatic service. I became Egypt's first Ambassador to the People's Republic of China in 1956 and then Ambassador to Italy in 1959. After leaving the diplomatic service, I became involved in the tourist industry. But the most exciting thing for me was rediscovering how to make papyrus, the writing paper of the Ancient Egyptians, because it pushed me into new and unexpected fields.

I first became interested in paper making while I was in China and thought that papyrus production would be a good cottage industry in Egypt. But no one knew how to make it, so I started doing research into it myself as a hobby.

I found that the Cyperus papyrus plant no longer grew in Egypt. It had once grown in abundance in the shallow, muddy water along the banks of the Nile. So I imported some from Sudan and started growing it on Jacob Island, in the Nile just south of Cairo. Then I started research into making the papyrus paper itself. It was difficult because the technique had died out after Chinese rice paper making methods were introduced in about the tenth century.

In Dr. Ragab's pharaonic village, actors demonstrate ancient fishing techniques.

When I finally produced the first piece of papyrus, I thought that the Government would want to develop the project, but it didn't; so in 1966 I set up the Papyrus Institute in Cairo to show people how it is made.

How is papyrus made? First, the outer part of the plant is cut away. Then the lower part of the stalk is cut into thin strips and soaked in water until it is soft. Then it is laid out on a piece of cloth and beaten. Finally it is covered by another piece of cloth and a block of stone and left to dry in the sun. After a couple of days you have a piece of papyrus! Although it is fairly simple, it is also very labor intensive and therefore expensive to make. But I found that it could be developed as an industry and papyrus paintings are now the number one tourist souvenir in Egypt. Papyrus pushed me into business!

Last year, I fulfilled another dream — the creation of a pharaonic village on

Dr. Ragab's pharaonic village provides a demonstration of how papyrus paper used to be made.

Jacob Island. The village is inhabited by about 300 Egyptian actors who practice agricultural and industrial activities, using the same tools and implements as those conserved in the Egyptian museum. There is a temple, the house of an ordinary peasant and the fully equipped villa of a nobleman. The villa shows how cultivated the ancient Egyptians were, even by modern standards. I have also planted trees and introduced birds typical of the ancient times.

But I have other plans too. I want to open a museum of paper and writing in Egypt, covering all the different techniques and materials from ancient times to the present. I already have a great deal of material, including a model of the Gutenberg press. I have plenty of ideas — all I need is time!

11

"Ignorant people are destroying the coral"

Tarek Amin, 26, known as "Pako" to his friends, is a scuba diving instructor in the Red Sea resorts of Sharm El Sheikh and Dahab in the southern Sinai.

I've always loved the sea. When I was 19, I was second in Egypt's Olympic class dinghy sailing and later on, while I was studying, I would get jobs abroad working on boats.

My father was a professor in electrical engineering so it was natural for me to study engineering too. But I hated it because of all the hard work! So I left after two years and went traveling. When I came back, I studied commerce instead. It was the only subject I could study on my own without attending lectures. I'd study for three months of the year and would spend the rest of my time down here around southern Sinai.

Before the Israelis occupied Sinai in 1967, there wasn't a tourist industry here, although an occasional diver or tourist would come on his own. The Israelis developed the Red Sea coast, from Sharm El Sheikh to Nuweiba. They built a few hotels and diving centers because water sports were becoming very popular. Egypt bought these facilities from the

Dahab on the Red Sea is being developed as a center for water sports.

Israelis when Sinai was handed back to Egypt under the Camp David Agreement in 1982.

When I first came here in 1982 the facilities were very basic. At first I got a job cleaning the beaches in return for food, but then I met a German scuba diver who offered to teach me how to dive if I'd help him. I gradually worked my way up to become a scuba instructor. Down here, we use a special method of instruction called PADI. This consists of several stages but you only teach a person what he has to know for each stage. This makes it very simple for anyone to learn the basics. Even so, new divers often get claustrophobic underwater and as an instructor, I have to be able to recognize any signs of panic, such as wide eyes or strange movements — it's a big responsibility for me.

One of the main reasons I decided to become a diving instructor was because I care about nature conservation. Most Egyptians are very ignorant in this respect — they come down here, kill the fish and steal the coral. They don't realize that the fish feed on the coral and vice-versa, that their actions may destroy the sea life forever. I try to teach people how to enjoy diving without destroying anything.

The Red Sea is extremely rich in plant and animal life. It is said to be one of the finest places in the world for diving. There are many good spots, but Ras Mohammad is reputed to be the best — it has been turned into a nature reserve. There are some special currents there so it gets an incredible variety of fish — napoleons, clowns, lions, jacks, spades, monterey and huge barracuda among others. I once saw about fifty hammerhead sharks — it was one day at the end of summer and they were migrating south. You never know what you may see. It's incredible! You get to know the regulars — there was a napoleon called George and a shark called Albi. You can feed some of them from your hand, but others, like stone and scorpion fish, are dangerous.

For me, the best place to see coral is Jackson Reef. Coral here grows 1–5 cm (2in) per year depending on the species, so you can understand what a tragedy it is for us when someone steals it.

There are many beautiful species of coral in the Red Sea.

"Cotton is the white gold of Egypt"

Wafaa Saad Khamis, 30, is married and has two young children. She tests the quality of cotton at the Cotton Arbitration and Testing General Organization (CATGO) in Alexandria, the heart of Egypt's cotton industry.

I got a degree in Agricultural Science at the University of Alexandria and have been working here for five years. Most married women work, so I'm not unusual. Cotton is one of the most important industries in Egypt. From 1850 until 1973, it was Egypt's main foreign exchange earner. Most of our industrial development has resulted from it, including the establishment of ginning, oilseed, textile and soap manufacturing industries. But with the need for more food production, the amount of cotton cultivation has decreased recently and more emphasis has been put on increased yield and quality per acre.

Cotton is grown with the help of irrigation in the Delta and the Dendera region of Upper Egypt. It takes about eight months to grow – from February until September – and is rotated with corn and clover. There are many different types of cotton, but Egypt produces the two finest types of cotton in the world, known as extra-long and long-staple. Although the world cotton market has been in a recession for several years, Egypt has suffered less than other countries because even in

Cotton samples are sent to the laboratory by growers and exporters for quality checks.

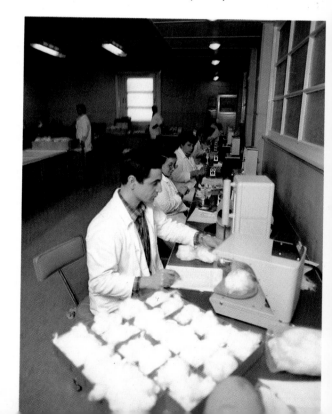

Wafaa tests the cotton for fineness and maturity.

the worst recession there is always a market for the best.

Because of heavy competition from abroad we have to be sure that our standards are maintained and that's where CATGO comes in. We train experts to grade cotton into different categories. We test the moisture content of cotton to determine its weight, and therefore its value, and test the physical properties of the cotton. We collect statistics on the industry as a whole and, finally, we act as a go-between for the producers and buyers in case of a dispute. I work in the cotton fiber-testing laboratory. The work is very technical, but basically we test the length, strength, fineness and maturity, as well as the content of foreign matter and the color and weight of the cotton fiber sent by export firms and those breeding new varieties of cotton. Our results are used to determine the best methods of processing the cotton and also to find out which of the new varieties is best.

In 1984, Egypt produced about 1.2 million tons of cotton. In the past, we exported most of it in its raw state, but over the last thirty-five years we have developed our own textile industry, so nowadays we only export about 40% of the raw cotton and process 60% ourselves. It is ironic that much of our own produce is of such high quality that it is too expensive for the home market. This means that we actually import some short staple cotton for use in this country.

Spinning techniques are also improving so that it is possible to get very good results from mixing the long staple with man-made fibers. I find it interesting to be involved in the constant development of this industry.

"We could not survive without the dam"

Ahmed Hassanain, 55, a civil engineer, has worked at the Aswan High Dam Authority since the initial construction phase in 1960.

Life in Egypt has always depended on the Nile River, but the river has invariably been very unstable. In some years the river would flood too much, causing terrible physical destruction, while in other years there would be drought and crops would be ruined, resulting in famine. So throughout history, there have been small-scale dams and irrigation projects. In 1902, the British finished the old Aswan Dam, which regulated the flow of the Nile during the year, but didn't have much storage capacity. Although the dam was raised twice to increase irrigation and hydroelectric capacity, it couldn't satisfy Egypt's growing need for both irrigated farmland and electrical power for industrialization.

So the Government decided to build the High Dam, 6 km (4 miles) upstream. This was done in two stages, from 1960–1971. In the first stage of construction, a diversion channel was cut through the east bank of the Nile. The rock which was removed in this process was dumped into the main riverbed to form a cofferdam — the foundation of the new dam. When this was completed in 1964, it forced the Nile waters to spill over into the diversion channel and through tunnels where it could be controlled to generate large amounts of electricity.

The control room of the Aswan High Dam power station determines the output of water through the twelve turbines.

The second stage of the project was the building of the High Dam itself. This is 110 m (364 ft) high and 3 km (two miles) wide at the top. When it was completed, the dam created Lake Nasser, which is 500 km (310 miles) long and stretches into the Sudan. The Nubian people who had been living in this area had to be evacuated and resettled. Various ancient temples, which would have been covered by the water, were moved to higher ground. These included the two great temples of Abu Simbel, which had originally been carved out of the rock itself.

The dam has provided Egypt with two vital resources: water and power. The dam can store surplus water over several years, balancing low floods against high. Due to drought in its upper reaches, the Nile recently fell to its lowest level in 350 years. Both Ethiopia and the Sudan suffered from terrible famine, and Egypt would have suffered the same fate if it had not been for the High Dam. However, irrigation projects using the waters of Lake Nasser have enabled us to increase Egypt's farmland area by 30 percent. At the same time, the generators of the High Dam have doubled the country's electricity supply.

As an engineer, I am concerned with any technical problems that crop up. The dam is made from many different materials, including granite, sandstone and clay. We have to keep a constant lookout for any cracks or weaknesses in the dam. We use very sensitive and accurate devices, which can measure any movement in the dam however slight.

The Aswan Dam provides Egypt with valuable water and hydroelectric power.

"People call me the queen of belly dance"

Nagwa Fouad started as a belly dancer in Cairo when she was only fifteen years old. She has since become a world-famous performer of this ancient Arabic dance form, and has performed in many foreign countries.

I ran away from my childhood home in Alexandria when I was thirteen because my father wanted me to marry an older relative whom I did not love. In the past this form of marriage was an accepted

Nagwa's floor-show is a combination of Egyptian and Turkish belly dancing.

practice, but now it is becoming more rare. I went to Cairo where my aunt took me into her house and I started looking around for a job. But finding a job was not easy, as I didn't have a college education. The most common thing for an uneducated girl to do would have been to take a job as a civil servant, working for a very low salary. I wanted something more exciting though, so I decided to have a look at the advertisements in the newspapers. Before long I had a job as a secretary working for one of Egypt's biggest show-business agents. My salary was the equivalent of about $1.10 a month!

I worked for him until I was fifteen but my desire to become "somebody" in my own right was growing all the time. I finally decided to start a career as a belly dancer in a cabaret called Sahara City. I had to have my papers falsified so that it would appear that I was sixteen years old, which was the minimum performing age. There are many belly dancers all over Cairo and most of them are very poorly

paid, but I was lucky enough to be recognized as a good dancer and I soon made it to the top. At the moment I am working in the nightclub in Cairo's Marriott Hotel. As the Marriott is one of the best in Egypt, I couldn't do much better! I suppose that a good belly dancer is the equivalent of a movie or pop star in the West.

The origin of belly dancing is not very clear, but I believe that it originated in Turkey and was introduced into Egypt during the Turkish occupation in the sixteenth century. In Upper Egypt we have our own dance tradition, based on Egyptian folklore, which is known as oriental dance. My show is a combination of the two and it is extremely popular among Arabs, both men and women.

As the name suggests, the most important movements in belly dancing take

It is traditional in Egypt for belly dancers to perform at wedding receptions.

place around the belly and the hips. The costume is made to accentuate these movements and the belly dance is accompanied by the music of several instruments: drums, flutes, violins and accordions. Often the orchestra consists of fifteen to twenty musicians. One of my performances lasts about one-and-a-half to two hours.

It is very difficult to become a good belly dancer. The most important thing is to have a special talent for it. You often see uninspired dancers, who only do it for money. The belly dancer must also have a special body – she must be supple and not too thin. Last but not least she has to work hard in order to perfect her art.

"A good Muslim must follow the Koran"

As Secretary General of the Higher Committee for Islamic Call, at Al-Azhar University in Cairo, 58-year-old Dr. Abdul Wadood Shalaby is one of the most highly respected Islamic leaders in the world.

Al-Azhar is the largest, oldest and most important Islamic university in the world, dating back to A.D. 975. The mosque was originally a place of worship and learning: lessons in Arabic, Islam and law were given to students sitting in small groups around the teacher on the floor of the mosque. Now that we have 10,000 boys and 8,000 girls studying here, that's no longer practical! Since 1961 it has

Muslims must pray five times every day.

been possible for students to study medicine, engineering and business (although they must also study Arabic and Islam), but some students still come to train purely as religious teachers. With over 50,000 mosques in Egypt alone, there is a great need for teachers.

Muslims come from all over the world to study here. If they are accepted they get free education, pocket money and accommodation in the Islamic Mission City. This currently houses 5,000 students, a different races, from seventy-two countries.

Good Muslims must follow the Koran – the teachings of God as revealed to His prophet Muhammad. They must observe five duties: they must bear witness that there is only one God – Allah – and that Muhammad is His prophet; they must pray five times every day; they must give alms to the poor, fast during the month of Ramadan and, if they are able to do so, make a pilgrimage to the holy city of Mecca in Saudi Arabia at least once in their lifetime.

A person is not a true Muslim unless he or she believes in all the prophets, including Moses and Jesus, and their scriptures. Islam is a religion of tolerance and peace, so we respect both Christians and Jews. One of the main differences between Islam and Christianity is that a Muslim believes in Jesus as a prophet but not as the son of God. Muslims believe that God's teachings were perfected in the Koran and that Muhammad was the last of His prophets.

Islam is a religion of life – it sets forth principles of human rights, freedom from discrimination, and rules for business, marriage, divorce and inheritance, among other things.

One of my main functions is to promote Islam, both inside and outside Egypt. There are more than 700 million Muslims

Al Azhar, built in A.D. 971, and is one of the best examples of Islamic architecture in the world.

in the world, but many are in the minority in their own country and suffer persecution. We try to help them with both material and moral support. A religious teacher must pass on his knowledge. I've traveled all over the world and held positions in England and Pakistan. For a while, I was also the chief editor of *Islam* magazine. I try to pass on my faith through conviction and teaching, not by force. Islam should not be used by fanatics for political ends. Here we welcome inquiry and discussion. At Al-Azhar we will always try to answer any question relating to Islam.

"I have delivered thousands of babies"

Om Aolooum, 63, has been a midwife since she was sixteen years old. She lives and works in the village of El Abaadeia in the oasis of El Faiyum.

When I was sixteen years old, the Government sent officers to my village looking for women to train as midwives. They approached me because my mother used to deliver babies although she never had any proper training. I'd been married since the age of fourteen, but as I wasn't very happy in my marriage, I decided to accept the offer of training. It meant that I had to go and live in El Faiyum, about 40 kilometers (25 miles) away, and go to a special school. The training lasted for about eighteen months – a year in school and six months practice. I was taught a few basic things like dealing with a fever and how to carry out the delivery itself. Then I came back to this village and have been living and working here ever since. I have six children of my own, delivered by my mother, so I know what it feels like to give birth!

When a woman starts to go into labor, her husband will come to get me, either on a donkey or by taxi. Not many people have their own cars. I have trained

Om Aolooum is frequently asked to examine sick children.

one woman in each of the surrounding villages to carry out uncomplicated deliveries, so I will only go to those places where there is a problem. If a particular delivery is very bad, I may give the woman some sugar tahini (a rich paste made from sesame seeds) to give her energy, or a local herbal plant, but I don't use any drugs. If there are more serious problems, I call the local doctor. In the past there were very few doctors in the area, but nowadays there is one in almost every village. In Egypt, the father is never present at the birth.

When the baby is born, I whisper some words of the Koran in its ear and then I lay it on the ground and ask the God of the Earth to look after him or her – that's an old tradition!

Sometimes there's a clash between modern methods and old traditions. I was taught that a baby should be washed immediately after the birth, but it's

Om Aolooum with one of the babies she delivered.

traditional not to do this. People differ, but some say that a baby shouldn't be washed until forty days after the birth! I can't force people to change – if I did and the child got sick, I would get the blame. I'm also supposed to put drops into the baby's eyes as soon as its head appears, but the liquid burns and the women here don't like me to do it, so what can I do?

If a new baby is ill, I will visit occasionally to check on its condition. The local doctor also has a clinic in the village. Normally the mother's female relatives help her and show her how to look after the new baby. On the third day the mother puts a dark powder called kohl around the baby's eyes, and on the seventh day there's a big party to celebrate. I'm always invited to that!

It's difficult for me to say if there are more babies being born today than forty years ago. I used to have to go to more villages, but I work in a smaller area than I used to. Some women use birth control but for the rest, it's all in the hands of Allah!

"22,000 ships use the canal each year"

Sixty-four-year-old Osman Ehsan has worked as a pilot on the Suez Canal since 1956, two years after the canal was nationalized by President Nasser. Before that he commanded a flotilla of minesweepers in the Egyptian Navy.

The Suez Canal is the third longest artificial international waterway in the world after the St. Lawrence Seaway in North America and the Baltic Sea Canal in the Soviet Union. It is considered to be

All the traffic going through the canal is monitored from a central control room at Ismailiya.

the main artery connecting Western Europe to South and East Asia. It is important because it allows ships to pass from the Mediterranean Sea to the Indian Ocean without having to make the long sea voyage around the southern cape of Africa.

The history of the canal is long and dramatic: the first known canal to connect the Mediterranean Sea and the Red Sea was dug about 4,000 years ago, using an ancient branch of the Nile River. Several other canals have been dug and used, but they all became silted up and forgotten. One of the most famous attempts was carried out by Napoleon's expedition to Egypt in 1798. He was very eager to have a canal built, but his chief engineer calculated wrongly that the level of the Red Sea was 10 m (33 ft) higher than the Mediterranean Sea and the project was canceled. The correct calculations were eventually made and in 1869 the Suez Canal was finally opened.

The canal was under English control

22,000 ships a year pass through the Suez Canal.

from 1882 until Egypt took it over in 1954. This resulted in an attack by the combined forces of Britain, France and Israel in October 1956. After twelve years of peace, the canal closed for eight years as a result of the Six-Day War in June 1967. It was eventually reopened in 1975.

The present-day canal has been made wider and deeper in order to give passage to modern day tankers. Today it can accommodate ships that draw up to 17 m (56 ft). It is 195 km (121 miles) long and it takes about twelve hours for a ship to pass through it.

As a pilot it is my responsibility to guide the ships safely through the canal.

They normally sail in convoys of five to ten at a time in each direction. There are several bypasses, where the canal has been widened to allow two convoys going in opposite directions to pass each other safely. There are also several safety and navigational systems that ensure the safety of the traffic on the canal. These include radar systems controlled by computer, but we still maintain our old, reliable telephone reporting system.

More than 22,000 ships use the canal every year, and this provides the third biggest source of foreign currency for Egypt, around $1,000 million per year. This figure is exceeded only by the oil sales and the savings of Egyptians working abroad.

25

"KIMA is the ancient word for 'black earth'"

Mohamed Khalil, 38, is the foreman of the nitrogen plant at KIMA fertilization factory in Aswan in Upper Egypt. He, his wife and four children live in a two-room apartment provided by the company.

When KIMA was opened in 1963, it was the largest fertilizer factory in Egypt. A hydroelectric power station had been built at the old Aswan Dam especially to provide the 250,000 kilowatts of electricity needed for the new plant. A town was built to provide housing, schools, health centers and leisure facilities for the 2,400 people who work here.

I was born in the Delta, but came here

KIMA provides cheap housing for its workers.

when I left school. The company provided a good training program: I would work a normal shift in the plant from 7:00 a.m. to 2:00 p.m. and would then study chemical engineering in the Higher Institute of Technology from 4:00 p.m. until 9:00 p.m. When I finally finished in 1980, I was put in charge of fifteen people in the nitrogen plant. I'm lucky because I only work on the day shift – most people have rotating shifts, as the factory is open night and day every day of the year.

In the past, when the Nile Valley was flooded every year, the flood waters would leave behind a layer of silt, which acted as a natural fertilizer. Since the New Aswan Dam was built, the waters of the Nile have been carefully controlled and there are no more floods. This means that people can farm three crops a year instead of only one, but it also means that the land needs more artificial fertilizers than before. Extra fertilizer is also required for the Government's vast land reclamation programs.

Here at KIMA, we produce about 280,000 tons of fertilizer per year. The basic elements required to make this are nitrogen and hydrogen. First, the hydrogen is produced by water electrolysis and nitrogen is extracted from the air by liquefaction and distillation. The hydrogen and nitrogen gases are then combined to make ammonia. Half of the ammonia is converted to nitric acid. The rest of the ammonia is mixed with this to form ammonium nitrate. This is mixed with limestone to produce calcium ammonium nitrate, the final product.

Different crops take different quantities of nitrates out of the earth. This means that various amounts of fertilizer are required in each area. The Government works out how much is required in each place and distributes it to the local

Mohamed checks the nitrogen level in one of the fertilizer silos.

agricultural cooperatives. It is then sold to the farmers at heavily subsidized rates. From Aswan, it is usually transported by train, although we do use some boats to carry it downstream as well.

This is a good place to work because there are lots of facilities. While an air-conditioned, two-room apartment anywhere else would cost at least E£100 ($73) a month, I pay only 50 piastres (37¢)! There is a health center, a subsidized food market and elementary, preparatory, and commercial and technical secondary schools. There are also very good sports facilities, including two swimming pools. I play soccer twice a week. Apart from that I watch television like everyone else.

"It's important for a girl to have a career"

Bassma Mohamed Aly El Sabae is 14 years old. She lives with her parents and older sister in Alexandria, where she attends the El Manar school.

My father is a commercial supervisor in a cotton dyeing company and my mother is a social worker. They thought that it was important for me to have a good education so they sent me here to El Manar. Although it is owned by the State, it was originally set up in 1925 by a Scot and has the characteristics of a private school. It charges fees and teaches the religions of Islam and Christianity (and is therefore closed on both Fridays and Sundays). The school puts great emphasis on the English language, and science and mathematics are taught in English from an early age.

The school is co-ed in the elementary and preparatory stages (for 6 to 15 year-

Bassma has eight hours of English every week.

olds) but is for girls only in the secondary stage (for 15 to 18 year-olds). School is compulsory for nine years, up to the end of the preparatory stage. Other schools put more emphasis on technical and commercial subjects than they do here, and there are also special technical and commercial secondary schools that train pupils for particular jobs. Those wishing to go on to college must achieve high grades at the end of the secondary stage. There are about 2,500 pupils here and about thirty girls go to college every year. Far more girls go to college now than in the past, but there are still far more boys than girls.

I'm in my last year of preparatory school, and I study Arabic, geography, history, religion, English, French, philosophy, math, botany and physics. I also take sports such as gym, volleyball and handball. My favorite subjects are math, geometry and English. I want to go to college to study electrical engineering because it's a respectable profession and it's important for a girl to have a career. I have to study English particularly hard because most scientific subjects are taught at college with English textbooks.

Most of the State schools are over-crowded and so pupils must share class-rooms. One group goes in the morning and the other goes in the afternoon. I don't think that it's because there are more children than in the past, but just that more of them are actually going to school. I have classes from 8:30 a.m. until 2:15 p.m. Then I go home for lunch and prayers. I have at least four hours of homework every day, but when I have time, I like drawing, sewing and watching television. I like cooking too, but my mother only lets me cook during the summer vacation as she thinks I should concentrate on my school work.

We have one week's vacation in January and four months off in the summer. Apart from that, we have some days off for festivals. In the summer we spend most of the time at home, but we also go to visit my mother's relatives in Cairo and have a beach vacation at Marsa Matrouh, which is very beautiful.

Alexandria, where Bassma lives, has many fine examples of Greek and Roman architecture.

"In some years it only rains for half a day"

Abdel Kader, 34, is a felah (farmer) and lives in Aezba Tunes, a small village in the oasis of El Faiyum. He is married and has six children.

I went to school for about a year when I was a boy, but after that I didn't have the time – I was too busy looking after the animals for my father. When I was twenty, my father gave me enough money to get married, but he's never given me anything else. He had four other boys and five girls to look after aside from me.

It's difficult to save money because I only make enough from farming to survive from day to day. Like many people from around here, I worked abroad on construction sites to earn enough money to buy a house and some land. It took me

Abdel's children often help him in the fields.

four years on and off, but then I was able to have a house built. It's made of stone with five rooms and one for the animals. I have a cow, a buffalo, five goats, ten sheep and two hectares (5 acres) of very good, fertile land.

Some people grow oranges here in the oasis, but I grow tomatoes, onions, corn and alfalfa as fodder for the animals, If I'm really busy, I rent a tractor from the village, but I prefer to work by hand, using a hoe, or wooden plow. The old fashioned way is better.

I sell the tomatoes directly to a merchant who takes them to Cairo. But for most products, I must deal with the local cooperative, which is in the next village. This sells us a certain amount of fertilizer cheaply. In return, we must sell the cooperative some of our produce. We may then do what we like with any surplus.

There's often a shortage of water, and because we depend on irrigation we argue about how the water should be distributed. The funny thing is that I live on the edge of a very large lake, but the land here is below sea level and the water is brackish, (slightly salty), fed partly by the Nile

Abdel worked abroad to save enough to have a stone house built for his family.

and partly by springs.

I have five sons and a daughter. I'd like them to have a good education but it's difficult because if the boys don't help me I have to hire laborers and I can't afford that. There are too many children here and not enough teachers, so the children are split into two groups. One group goes to school in the morning and the other goes in the afternoon. That helps me because it means that there is always at least one child to help me at any time. Some people refuse to send their children to school during the day so a special evening class has been set up.

We have no electricity in the village — only oil lamps — so we tend to get up and go to bed early. I get up at about 6:00 a.m. have breakfast, pray and start working in the fields at about 7:00 a.m. I work until 5:00 p.m. with three hours off in the middle of the day when it's usually too hot to work. I'm lucky because I have very fertile land — some others have to work much harder for the same results.

"We use nets and traps to catch the fish"

Mohamed Gaber El Seid, 51, is a fisherman on Lake Mariout, just south of Alexandria in the Nile Delta. He is also a Sheik Sayadin (spokesman) for about 500 other fishermen.

The fishing boats are in constant use twenty-four hours a day.

I started fishing with my father when I was twelve so I have spent most of my life on the waters of Lake Mariout. The lake is in the Nile Delta, separated from the sea by a narrow strip of land and fed by the Nile River, so the water is brackish, not salty. There are about 5,000 fishermen altogether on the lake, owning about 2,000 boats among them. A fisherman will normally go out for eight hours at a time. When a boat's owner isn't fishing, then his son or a friend will take it out, so it's in use twenty-four hours a day. Some of the fishermen work in offices during the day and fish only at night. But every man has his own tackle and will repair his own nets. It's also necessary to have a fishing license from the Government.

Lake fishing isn't like sea fishing, so although we are very close to the Mediterranean Sea here, a man will either fish the sea or the lake, but never both. The techniques are different. Lake Mariout is only one or two meters (3–6 ft) deep at any point so we usually use nets and traps to catch the fish. In fact it's easier to catch fish in bad weather because they stay near the bottom. On a good day, I may catch 5–7 kilos (11–15 lbs) of fish. About 90 per-cent of the fish here are tilapia; 8 percent are catfish and 2 percent are of other types. One type of tilapia has been named after the Nile River because it is so com-mon here – *Tilapia nilotica*. They, are quite small, the largest weighing only about 1 kilo (2 lb) but they are very tasty.

When we bring our catch back to the shore it is auctioned. The buyers then take it to the fish market in Alexandria. Most fishermen here belong to a coopera-tive which provides various benefits, such as cheap loans and duty free equip-ment in return for a small annual fee. Until recently, we have had to sell a cer-tain proportion of our catch to the cooperative at cheap rates, but we refuse to do this anymore, so everything is sold at the market rate.

When I was a boy, the lake was much bigger than it is now and there were more

fish. In the 1950s, the lake covered more than 5,000 hectares (12,400 acres) but now it's only 3,300 hectares (8,170 acres). Gradually more and more land has been reclaimed for agriculture. The Govern-ment has started a number of fish farms to increase production, but this doesn't help us. The lake is also becoming more and more polluted because of the industriali-zation going on around Alexandria.

There are about seven fishing com-munities here and each one has an elected *sheik sayadin*, or spokesman, who is then appointed by the State. He pro-vides a link between the State and the fishermen and mediates when there are problems. I was elected by my commun-ity and I represent about 500 fishermen. I'd like to do something about the pollu-tion before it's too late.

I have three daughters and four sons. None of my sons are fishermen, but I don't mind. They all went to school and later became Government employees. They have more security than I had and some say that it's a better life. But I like to be outside – I could never have worked in an office.

Lake Mariout is very marshy, so Mohamed can use only a small boat.

"We must make use of our rich heritage"

Shahira Mehrez, 42, is trying to prevent traditional Egyptian arts and crafts from dying out. She and fourteen other women run a chain of shops selling antiques and traditional peasant dresses commissioned from all over Egypt.

I come from a landowning family. Before the Revolution in 1952, it was considered a waste of time to educate a wealthy girl. It was assumed she would marry a boy with a similar background and would never have to work.

But after the Revolution, the Government confiscated a lot of land and broke up the large landowning families. It also nationalized a lot of related industries, such as cotton and controlled the prices. Suddenly, land no longer provided sufficient income and people realized that women might have to work too. Thus, women of my generation were automatically given a good education, while those only five or six years older had to fight to get one.

After college I studied Islamic art history and through this I met the architect, Hassan Fathi, who was interested in traditional methods of building. He designed my apartment. It is perfectly suited to a modern way of life, yet incorporates traditional features, such as a fountain courtyard and *mashrabeyyah* screens — these are wooden screens made with intricate latticework. In the old days when women weren't allowed out of the house, they could sit

Shahira lives in a modern apartment, which incorporates traditional features.

34

behind these screens and look out with-out being seen. Apart from their decora-tive effect, I have them for a far more prac-tical reason: the holes allow air to flow through the house, which is very nice in the summer.

I also worried about the way so many customs were dying out. One day, I was discussing this with some friends and we decided to do something about it. We started with clothes. I had started collect-ing old Bedouin dresses when I was six-teen because I thought they were so attractive. Then I discovered that in the past, every village produced its own special type of dress and that it was still possible to find them in the markets. We also looked for people who could still

Every village in Egypt has its own traditional dress design.

remember the designs that had died out. At first, people were offended, because they thought that we were mocking them, but they gradually realized that we were genuinely interested.

We started selling the dresses once a week, then three times and then we had to open a shop. Now we have several shops and sell many different things, including antiques, pottery, carpets and jewelery. I like being involved with crea-tive people and I hope that I can encour-age people to make use of our very rich heritage instead of relying on cheap copies of Western designs.

"I'm proud to serve my country"

Abdul El Hakeem, 20, was brought up as a farmer in Assyut, but at present he is a soldier in the Egyptian army. He is stationed at El Kharga in the Western Desert.

Every man has to do military service unless he is an only son or unfit for duty. The period depends on whether or not he has had a higher education, and it may last for anything from a few months to three years.

My father is a farmer and I was born and brought up in Assyut in the Nile Valley. As I had to work on the farm, I never went to school. That's usual for farmers – a son learns everything he needs to know from his father. I like farming, but I don't mind being in the army for a while – I'm proud to be able to serve my country. Besides, every man should be able to defend both himself and his family. Egypt has had to defend itself many times in the last twenty years. The only way for a country to develop is to have peace. I can't imagine fighting in a war but I would be happy to defend my country – I don't think I would be afraid.

I've been in the army for six months now and have another two-and-a-half years to go. I've been stationed here in El

Soldiers guard important buildings.

El Kharga oasis is of great strategic importance to the Egyptians.

Kharga from the beginning and I will stay here for the whole of my military service. For the first four months, I had to go through basic training, doing various drills and exercises and learning how to use firearms. I found the discipline difficult at first, but I'm used to it now. It's a good life – you get clothes, food and pay and don't have any worries. I do miss my family though – this is the first time I have been away from home.

Egypt has feared invasion through the desert ever since ancient times. El Kharga is the southernmost of several oases in the Western Desert and is particularly important because of its position at the junction of a number of caravan routes crossing the Sahara. This line of oases has traditionally constituted the defensive line of Egypt from the west and

the south. Communications between the oases are better now than they used to be, but the oases are still rather isolated places.

The army also plays an important role in civilian life. At the moment I am guarding an administrative building. This is basically a police function but we carry out many police duties here. I wear a special badge on my cap to show this. We also help out on much larger projects, such as building bridges or other construction work. It just depends on what is needed. If someone is in trouble, the army will always try to help out. Sometimes soldiers are used to man fire engines or help with hospital transportation.

"I see my family once every two months"

Mohammad El Zayd Ahmet, 48, has been the captain of a felucca, transporting sugarcane on the Nile River, for the last sixteen years.

My grandfather and my father were farmers and I was brought up on a small farm in Nag Hammadi, in the Nile Valley. I was also a farmer for a while, but then I started working on the riverboats and became a captain. Now I work for a sugar factory, transporting sugarcane. The factory owns five boats. In the past, all the feluccas had sails and some of them still do, but the feluccas belonging to the factory are pulled by a motor boat. You can load more sugarcane in the boats if they don't have sails and although they still move slowly, they don't have to depend on the wind.

Egypt produces over nine million tons of sugarcane per year, most of which is grown in the Nile Valley and Upper Egypt. Unfortunately, this amount only provides about 70 percent of Egypt's total needs, so we still have to import some. It's a very important crop, but takes up a lot of space and is fairly labor intensive. It would be difficult to increase production without heavy investment and

The Nile River provides the best means of taking the heavy and bulky sugarcane from the fields to the refinery.

extensive irrigation.

Sugarcane is also very heavy and bulky to transport. The farmers bring it down to the loading dock by whatever means they can — by truck, donkey or camel. Camels are good because they are so strong. It takes us about four hours to load the boats with the cane and then another three hours to take it up to the factory. At the factory, molasses is extracted from the sugarcane. Then, about every two months, we transport the molasses downstream to Nag Hammadi. That trip takes about five days. We buy fish from passing fishermen and sleep on the boats.

My wife and two children live in Nag Hammadi, but most of the time I'm based at Luxor, about 120 km (75 miles) farther south, so I only get to see them about once every two months when we take the molasses down there. It's a tough life, but I need the money to give my children a better one. I get E£100 ($73) per month and send half of that home to my wife. My daughter has just been married — that cost me E£1500 ($1100), so now I only have my son to think of. I don't want him to be a farmer or a sailor like me — I want him to go to college and get a good education. That's what you need if you want a decent job in today's society.

The sugarcane is often carried to the felucca by donkey.

"I pack dates in winter, onions in summer"

Aida Hassan Hamed, 19, works in a date and onion packaging factory in El Kharga, an oasis in the Western Desert, where she lives with her parents and two unmarried brothers.

Like most people here, my father is a farmer, working on a Government farm. I'm one of nine children. I have four married and two unmarried brothers and two married sisters. My sisters are both housewives with children. I would like to be married too, but I hope to have only two sons and would like to continue to work.

I've been working here in the factory for a year now, ever since getting my school certificate at the agricultural school in El

The dates are cleaned and sorted before they are packed.

Kharga. It's a small factory, with about 200 employees, divided into three shifts. I always work on the morning shift, from 7:00 a.m. to 3:00 p.m. That means I must get up early as I live in the old part of town, 3 km (2 miles) away and have to walk here. During the day, I get thirty minutes break so I always bring cheese and eggs from home. I can also eat as many dates as I like while I'm working!

The date palms are very important to us. They start producing fruit after five to eight years and give the best crop when they are fifteen to twenty years old, but they can still produce fruit after one hundred years. They need quite a lot of water. It only rains about once every fifteen years, but there are huge reservoirs of underground water. We have wells and pumps and can use this water to irrigate the palm trees. A palm tree needs 9 liters (2 gallons) of water per week.

We don't use just the fruit of the date palm, we also use the leaves to make roofs for the houses, especially those in the old town where houses are still made of mud brick.

The dates grow during the summer and are harvested in September and October. They used to be packed entirely by hand, but then the Government set up this factory in 1963. So the dates are now brought here for packing before being sent to Cairo and Alexandria for distribution.

In the factory they are first put into a steam compressor, to kill germs. Then they are washed, pressed and packed. We remove the stones from some of them and insert almonds, which we import from the U.S. We pack about 15 tons of dates every winter from September to April. During the summer, we pack dried onions instead. Some of these are exported internationally. They don't taste

El Kharga is irrigated by water pumped from underground streams.

as good as the dates!

There are other girls of my age working here and I enjoy their company. I think that it's important for people to work. I need the money, but at the same time I like to think that I am helping my country to develop.

We're lucky in El Kharga because there's very little unemployment, unlike other parts of the country. There are many Government programs to persuade people to come here from the overcrowded Nile Valley. There's a glass factory, a phosphate mine, carpets, poultry farms and many new agricultural projects.

"Our lives are bound by very simple rules"

Soleman Eid Soleman, 32, is a member of the Bedouin Muzeina tribe of the Southern Sinai. He is a successful businessman, but he still leads a semi-nomadic way of life.

There are about 100,000 Bedouin in Sinai, of whom about 4,000 to 5,000 belong to the Muzeina tribe. Although we are nomadic, we always move within the southern part of the Sinai, around Sharm el Sheikh, Dahab and Nuweiba.

"Bedouin" means "desert dweller" and traditionally Bedouins are nomads, moving from place to place depending on the availability of water and pasture for their animals. Here in Southern Sinai, we've always done some fishing as well as farming. The women usually look after the babies, the animals, the cooking and housekeeping in the village, while the men fish or do business. We have much more money than in the past because there's been a lot of development in the Sinai: oil wells, construction and tourism provide many business opportunities. Some Bedouin have taxis, some work for the oil companies and so on. Life is changing. Some of the younger men are beginning to settle down in one place, but the older ones have to keep moving.

My father was a fisherman, so I became one too. I worked for a while on the big fishing boats in Israel and saved some money, then I started my own business. Now I have a cafe and a supermarket in Sharm el Sheikh. I have a fishing boat too, although a friend does the fishing for me.

Bedouins use both traditional and modern forms of transportation.

I try to work as little as possible! But I still have to make sure that everything is run the way it should be.

I have a big villa in Suez and a small house in Sharm (where my two wives live). But I also have a home in a small Bedouin village, which moves around every one or two months: this is where my mother lives. In the winter we stay down near the sea, while in the summer we move up into the mountains. We have seven cars and four pick-up trucks between us so we load everything into them and move on to the next place. Our homes are made of wood and corrugated iron — not many people use tents anymore.

Until about twenty years ago, everyone used camels for transportation. But then, under the Israelis, we started using trucks and realized how much more practical they were. Nowadays most Bedouin use them.

Another development is that we don't have to move in search of water — we can fill up from a water tanker that comes to

Bedouin women still wear traditional clothing and jewelery.

Sharm. Some things get easier.

I have eight children and I'd like them all to have a good education. I never went to school and never learned to write although I learned to speak Hebrew and English because I needed to do so. I may be successful but it hasn't always been easy — people want too many written documents. Among Bedouins, a written contract is never needed — a man's word is his honor. If there is a disagreement within a tribe, the Sheik decides. If there's a problem between tribes, then all the Sheiks of the tribes involved get together to judge the matter. Hospitality is very important to a Bedouin. If a stranger comes to him, he must treat him better than he would a friend, providing food, tea or water and shade from the sun.

Despite modernization, our lives are bound by very simple rules. Compared to people in the cities, we have few problems.

"Our designs come from life in the oasis"

Fatma Shorbagy, 24, has been making carpets in a small factory in El Kharga for the last ten years. She lives with her mother and two married brothers with fourteen children.

I started here when I left elementary school at the age of fourteen. One of my sisters had been working here and I liked the idea of making carpets. Besides, I had to earn some money to help my family. My sister left the factory when she got married, but I'm still here, along with about thirty other girls. I'm one of the oldest and most experienced in the factory so I usually train the new girls. It's possible to do simple work after a week, but it takes about eighteen months to become really good at it. As we are paid by the amount of work that we do, it's important to be able to work quickly! It takes me about twenty-four days to make a carpet 6 m (20 ft) long, so I make an average of about E£1.5 ($1.10) per day.

The carpets are all made of wool. We get the wool from Assyut in the Nile Valley, where there has always been a lot of sheep farming.

Two or three girls usually work on one carpet at a time.

We use upright looms and normally two or three girls work on one carpet at a time. We use traditional designs – they all come from the life we see around us. They are very simple; the small ones perhaps depicting a camel or a donkey, the more elaborate ones showing the various stages of date harvesting with donkeys, camels, people and lots of date palms. The designs are drawn on graph paper and then copied onto the loom. I do many of my own designs here.

The Government set up this factory in 1965. In addition to the carpets, it also produces pottery and kilims (small rugs). The kilims are made by six deaf and mute boys.

I start work at 6:00 a.m. and leave at midday, six days a week, with Friday off. In the summer it is far too hot to work in the afternoon. When I get home, I have to help my mother because there's always lots of work to do.

My father died in 1982 and as he didn't work for the Government, my family didn't get any pension, just a small amount of money from the social welfare. It's been very difficult for us to live as we are a big family. My mother and I live with two of my married brothers and their wives and families. They each have seven children so there are twenty-one people in the household!

I want to be able to contribute more to the household so I am studying at home to do the preparatory school exams. I can borrow all the necessary books from the library and get some help from a teacher. When I have passed, I can get a Government post at the carpet factory on a fixed salary so I will earn much more than I do now. Boys are usually given a better education than girls because they are expected to support a household, whereas many girls stop working when

In another oasis nearby, the main income comes from pottery.

they get married. But I want to contribute something to the country and help it to develop. I would want to continue even if I was married, because I enjoy working. Most girls are married by the time they're twenty but I'll wait – I don't want to make a mistake.

"Most of the tombs have been robbed"

Mohamed Nasr, 44, is an Egyptologist and Director of Antiquities on Luxor's West Bank, the site of the tombs and temples of the ancient capital of Thebes, dating back more than 3,000 years.

I'm responsible for all the excavation work on the West Bank. This includes the Valley of the Kings, the Valley of the Queens, the tombs of the Nobles and the workmen and the mortuary temples of Seti I, Hatshepsut, Ramses II and III among others. Excavation and restoration work is going on continuously — aside from our own works, there are ten foreign missions, which I have to both control

Mohamed's favorite tomb is that of Sennutem, because it depicts scenes of everyday life and an ordinary man's vision of paradise.

and assist. I also help both individual experts and tourists. Over one thousand tourists visit this area daily during the winter. The fees they pay go toward our restoration and maintenance work.

In ancient times, Egypt was divided into two separate kingdoms, Upper and Lower Egypt. Thebes became important as a capital city after the unification of the two kingdoms and because of its central position on the Nile. Its greatest period was from 1570 to 1090 B.C. Burials began at the Valley of the Kings during the reign of Tuthmosis I (1525–1495 B.C.) and most of the subsequent pharaohs of that period were also buried there. Unfortunately, almost all the tombs were robbed, so all that remains in most cases are the paintings on the walls. The one great exception is the tomb of Tutankhamun, the only pharaoh's tomb ever to be found intact. Tutankhamun was only about nineteen when he died and his tomb was unfinished. He was unimportant compared to other pharaohs and his tomb was soon covered by the debris of the much grander tomb of Ramses VI. When it was finally rediscovered in 1922, it was found to contain more than 5,000 fabulous objects, originally placed in the tomb to provide the pharaoh with everything he might require in the afterlife.

Religion played an important part in the lives of the ancient Egyptians. They worshipped a number of different gods, such as Keb, the god of the earth, Nut the goddess of heaven and Osiris the god of the underworld. All these gods were descended from the most important one of all, the Sun god, who appeared in a number of different forms and names.

Some gods had human bodies but animal heads. Thoth, the god of wisdom and truth, had the head of an ibis, and Anubis, who assisted Osiris as judge of the dead and guardian of the tombs, had the head of a jackal. Since people thought that death was a continuation of life, they spent their lives preparing for it. Upon death, the deceased and his spirit would travel to the next world, where his pleas that he had not sinned would be judged by Osiris and his assistants. His heart would be weighed on a scale of justice with a feather (the symbol of truth) used as a balance.

While the pharaonic tombs are very imposing and stately, I personally prefer some of the private tombs such as that of Sennutem, a servant of a pharaoh, where the paintings are very basic, depicting scenes of everyday life. It is from such paintings that we learn most about everyday life in ancient Egypt.

The tomb of King Tutankhamun contained more than 5,000 objects when it was discovered in 1922.

"The bridegroom must pay a dowry"

Badia Osman Soliman, 31, runs the Habu Hotel on Luxor's West Bank with her husband, Sobhi, to whom she has been married for seventeen years. They have two sons and one daughter.

My father was a farmer and I was born here on the West Bank. My husband, Sobhi, used to play with me when I was a child. When I was thirteen he asked my parents if he could marry me. He was twenty-nine then and I thought that was very old. I used to call him uncle! Sobhi also came from a farming family, but he'd already bought the Habu Hotel, so I knew that it would be good for me to marry him.

It's traditional here for the bride's family to provide all the furnishings for the

The hotel is busiest between April and October when the weather is cooler.

Badia buys bread for the hotel from her next-door neighbor, who bakes bread for the whole village.

new home. The bridegroom must pay a dowry to the girl's father, give her gold jewelery and also provide her with somewhere to live. We were engaged for a year, while we waited for a new house to be built next to the hotel, and all the other preparations to be made. I was fourteen when we finally got married.

Now I have one daughter, Hala and two sons, Mohamed and Adam. Three is enough! I don't want my daughter to marry before she is twenty. I was too young – I wanted to play, have a bicycle, do all the other things that a young girl does. But instead I had to grow up quickly to look after my husband, the house and the hotel. I'd like my children to go to, college, *Inshallah* (God willing)!

The modern city of Luxor is on the east bank of the Nile, but many of the ancient temples and tombs are on the west bank. People come from all over the world to see them. Although Hotel Habu is very simple, it has a magnificent view over the temple of Medinet Habu, the last great pharaonic temple, built by Ramses III.

I am always very busy looking after the hotel, my home and my children, but I prefer things this way. I employ five people including a cook, but I have to cope with the housekeeping, the food and the finances myself when Sobhi is away. Because of the tourists, everything is very expensive, so I go to other towns to buy meat. I also keep ducks and chickens so that I have both meat and eggs. The bread comes from the woman who lives next door. She has an oven and bakes bread for everyone in the village. I also get milk and vegetables locally – all the fruit and vegetables that we need can be grown here in the Nile Valley.

The high season is from October until April when the weather is a little cooler. I like looking after the guests and meeting people from all over the world. I have made many friends. When I have time I also like to visit my local friends and family. While I am at home I can wear any clothes that I like, but when I go out I wear something black with a veil over my head. I also wear all my jewelery – it's a tradition in the village, but I don't think that my daughter will continue it.

"Business isn't as good as it used to be"

Mustafa Mohammad Hamama, 29, owns a shop selling copper and brass in the heart of Cairo's medieval bazaar, known as Khan el Khalili.

Mustafa started working in his father's shop when he was seventeen.

My father bought this shop in Khan el Khalili in 1956 for E£30 ($22) – today it must be worth at least E£30,000 ($22,000)! Of course, money was worth more in those days – I remember that as a child I could buy twenty eggs for 1 piastre (less than a cent at today's rate of exchange) while today I have to pay 10 piastres (7¢) for just one egg!

I have three brothers and four sisters so there were a lot of mouths to feed. My father used to sell household goods, but he made barely enough for us all to survive. On some days he would make only about E£1.5 ($1.00 at today's rate) profit. I started helping him in the shop when I was seventeen. I wanted him to sell copper and brass and try to get some of the tourist trade, but he wasn't interested. Then one day I bought a brass teapot for 50 piastres (37¢) and my father let me put it into the shop. The next day, I sold it for E£15 ($12)! My father was amazed that I could make such a profit, so after that, he sold only copper and brass and started to do really well. When my father died I took over the business with one of my brothers, although the profits are shared out among all of us.

Khan el Khalili is in one of the oldest parts of Cairo. The market grew up around an inn in the fourteenth century. It has always attracted a lot of foreign merchants. You can get almost anything here, from perfume and jewelery, to leather, fabrics and souvenirs. It's a very picturesque part of Cairo, full of narrow, winding streets, mosques and old houses.

Business isn't as good as it used to be. Between 1973 and 1978 we were so busy we didn't have time to eat! There weren't many shops that sold copper and brass, so we were very popular with the tourists. Copperware and brassware made nice souvenirs because the craftsmanship was

There is a wide selection of copper and brass for sale in Mustafa's shop.

good, the objects were useful (teapots, bowls, plates and tables, among other things), and they still had an oriental flavor. But then other people caught on and now there are five times as many stores selling the same kind of goods.

Aside from the competition, I think that the nature of tourism has changed. There used to be quite a lot of individual travelers, who would spend a lot of time browsing in the bazaar. But nowadays, most people come in groups and go on bus tours of Cairo. People don't have as much money as they used to. The buses only stop for five or ten minutes, so people don't even have time to look around anymore.

"Life is not quite the same"

Mrs. Ragabia-Bastawy is a Nubian and was born in the village of Abu Simbel in 1905. When the village was covered by the waters of Lake Nasser, after the New Aswan Dam was built, she and her family were moved to a new town, 64 km (40 miles) north of Aswan.

I have very happy memories of the old Nubia, which lay along the Nile Valley between Aswan and the Sudan. We had a large house on the banks of the Nile, with views of the river on one side and date palms and the desert on the other. In 1963, the Government sacrificed Nubia when the Aswan High Dam was being built. They moved forty-three villages here to new Nubia so that the old valley could be flooded by the waters of Lake Nasser. They built new stone houses and every village kept its own name, but it wasn't the same. For one thing, we had very fertile land before, which was renewed every year by mud from the Nile's flood waters. Here we have irrigated land, away from the Nile, which must be fertilized because it isn't naturally rich. Old Nubia lay on the main trading route between Egypt and Sudan, so we used to do a lot of trading. Here, we only have local trade. My family came from a village called Abu Simbel, so we moved to a new Abu Simbel here, but the great temple which once lay opposite our village, has been moved to a different place over 200 kilometers (125 miles) to the south!

In old Nubia, everyone was involved with dates – it's said that over 20 million date palms have been covered by Lake Nasser. My husband had a big date shop

Mrs. Ragabia-Bastawy was moved to a new Government-built village when her old home was covered by the waters of Lake Nasser.

and sent dates to Aswan, Cairo, Alexandria and other cities. When we were moved here, he was given a new shop next to our house, but it's a general store and so dates went out of our lives.

People's attitudes have changed too. In old Nubia, families used to live together in large houses, with maybe sixteen or eighteen people in one household. When we cooked a meal, all our neighbors would be invited. They would invite us the next time. But here, families live in small groups and eat alone. People don't help each other as they used to. The only time people get together as in the old days is for weddings and funerals, when the whole village eats together and gets involved.

Some things haven't changed. There is no crime here and any problems are

Mrs. Ragabia-Bastawy with a few members of her large family.

solved by the Elder of the village, elected by its members. We still have special customs for marriage and funerals.

Some things are better. In the past, we had no television and no electricity – we only had gas lamps. Here we have electricity because of the High Dam. We have also had television since 1964. People are richer than in the past as many men work abroad and send their earnings home. We have radios and refrigerators that we never had before. Education and the health service are much better than in the past. So the younger generation doesn't mind that we were moved. It is just not quite the same to those of us who can remember life as it was before.

53

"I sail the best cruise boats on the Nile"

Fathi Ahmed Abdel Nabi is the captain of Sheraton's *Aton* cruise ship – very different from the simple riverboats he used to sail with his father.

I know the Nile River like the back of my hand. A big company like the Sheraton could employ someone with all the paper qualifications in the world, but they prefer a local man like me, who has learned about the river by experience. The *Aton* was built in Norway and has the most modern and sophisticated equipment available for navigating, but I don't need it. Even so, I have to be careful sometimes, because the riverbed is changing all the time. It is very shallow in certain places, but I know what is happening by the way it looks — that only comes with experience.

My father had his own boat and used to transport sugarcane and barley. I helped him part-time while I was at school and then joined him full-time from the age of eighteen when I left preparatory school.

My brother was also a sailor, working for a company that transported oil and other raw materials. He managed to get me a job with them, and so I started working with him. After four months I was promoted to first mate and worked in that position for two years. Then the company promoted me to captain and gave me a boat. I transported oil and other raw materials for them, sailing from Alexandria to Aswan. I worked for them for

The Sheraton cruise boat is equipped with the most modern, sophisticated equipment for navigation, but Fathi seldom uses it because he knows the river by heart.

54

The Sheraton cruise boat shares the Nile River with more traditional forms of transportation.

twenty-two years.

Then I got the chance to work for the Sheraton on the *Aton*, which had just been built. The Sheraton has four boats at the moment, although they are having more built. They're basically first class floating hotels; the *Aton* has eighty-two cabins, including two suites. The boats cruise for five to seven days at a time, between Luxor and Aswan in Upper Egypt. We stop at the most interesting places on the way, such as Esna, Edfu and Kom Ombo, where our guides take the guests to see all the magnificent temples. Between stops, they can relax on deck, sunbathe, swim and watch the scenery go by — it's a beautiful trip.

At the end of the tourist season I usually have to sail the *Aton* back to Cairo, so that any maintenance work can be carried out there. Then we take a special ten-day cruise, which is a nice change, although it's very hot at that time of the year.

Things have changed a lot on the Nile River. It's much more crowded than it used to be, with a lot more sailboats, motorboats and cruise boats. Thirty-five years ago, there were hardly any tourist boats — the Royal Family had one and there was one other, but that was basically it. Now there are more than ninety different tourist boats concentrated between Luxor and Aswan — the most interesting and beautiful part of the river. Some of these are badly maintained, so I'm proud to be working on one of the best.

"Cairo is the media center of he Middle East"

In January 1983, Dr. Mamdouh El Beltagui, 46, was appointed by the President of Egypt to be Chairman of the State Information Service in Cairo.

My father was a judge, so it was natural for me to become a lawyer. After obtaining my license, I worked in the Ministry of Justice as District Attorney and Public Prosecutor for nine years. But after that, I decided to change direction and went to Paris, where I obtained doctorates in economics and political science. I was Minister Counselor for Information in Paris for seven years before being made Chairman of the State Information Service here in Cairo.

I am responsible for State Information both within and outside the country. We have forty offices in forty capitals abroad and fifty-five internal centers. These

The People's Assembly in Cairo.

cover mainly economic, social and political issues through the use of written material, films, videos and conferences so my work is extremely varied.

Cairo has become the main regional platform for the media in the Middle East. This means that all the most important newspapers, magazines, television and radio networks have representatives here. I deal with 400 permanent correspondents and 1,500 passing correspondents and writers every year.

Cairo is a very important press center because it is in a convenient geographical position and has all the latest media technology. But I believe that the main reason for its development is the freedom of the press here and the stability and democratic nature of our political constitution.

Egypt has a republican, multi-party political system and a democratic socialist economic system. The main legislative body is the People's Assembly, consisting of 350 members, elected by the people of Egypt by secret ballot every five years.

The People's Assembly approves draft laws, the general policy and budget of the

Dr. Mamdouh El Beltagui deals with 400 permanent newspaper correspondents living in Cairo.

State and the State's general plan of economic and social development. It also selects a President to act as Head of State, whose nomination must be submitted to public referendum. The President has a term of six years and he appoints the Council of Ministers to govern the country. The President and the Ministers thus carry out the executive authority of the State. The Ministers are collectively responsible to the People's Assembly for their actions.

Apart from the People's Assembly, there is another important advisory body known as the Shura Council. The Shura Council is chiefly concerned with safeguarding the democratic socialist system in Egypt. Two thirds of its members are elected by direct secret public balloting, while the other third is appointed by the President.

Local administration is dealt with through government, district, city and village councils, which are spread throughout the country.

Facts

Capital city: Cairo (population 12 million)

Principal language: Arabic and classical "fusha" Arabic are combined by the Egyptians to form their living language – "Al-lughat ad-daariga." Many educated Egyptians also speak French and English.

Currency: 100 piastres = 1 Egyptian pound (E£); 1.37 Egyptian pounds = about $1.

Religion: The predominant religion is Islam, but there are over 6,500,000 Christians (Muslim 94 percent, Christian 6 percent). The chief Muslim religious authorities in Egypt are *Sheik el Gami el Ashar* and the *Mufti Gumhuriya Misr al Arabiya.* There is also a minority of Greek Orthodox, Roman Catholics, Armenians and Protestants. By 1968, nearly all of the Jews in Egypt had left the country.

Population: There are approximately 44.67 million people in Egypt (1982). There are three population groups. The largest is the Hamito-Semite group known in the rural districts as Fellahin (fellah meaning plowman or tiller of the soil). Secondly, there are the Bedouin or Nomadic Arabs of the Libyan and Arabian deserts, of whom about one seventh are real nomads, and the remainder are tent-dwellers living on the outskirts of the cultivated end of the Nile Valley and the Fayum. The third group are the Nubian people of the Nile Valley between Aswan and Wadi-Halfa. They are a people of mixed Arab and Negro blood. The Bedouins and Nubians are Muslims.

Climate: Hot with low humidity. The midsummer months are very hot and dry, while the rest of the year is hot with a little rain. The hottest month is July, with temperatures ranging from 21–36°C (70–97°F). The coldest month is January, with temperatures ranging from 8–18°C (46–64°F). The driest months of the year are July and August. The wettest month is December with a monthly average of 5mm (.2 in) rainfall.

Government: Legislative power is held by the People's Assembly. The Assembly nominates the President, who is elected by popular referendum for six years and is eligible for reelection. President Muhammad Husni Mubarak has been in power since President Sadat was assassinated on October 6, 1981. Egypt became a republic in June 1953, following the removal from power of King Farouk in July 1952, and his son in 1953.

Industry: Agriculturally based industries, such as textiles and food-processing, form an important part of Egyptian industry. There are heavy industry plants at the Helwan iron and steel complex with a further steel plant being built at Alexandria; aluminum is produced at the Nag Hammadi plant using imported bauxite. The growth of heavy industry in Egypt and the spread of electricity to rural areas has led to the development of more power stations. Egypt's energy program includes the construction of hydroelectric, nuclear and gas power stations. Egypt is also developing its social hygiene facilities, including one of the world's largest sewage disposal projects – the Greater Cairo Waste Water Project.

The Media: An organized press in Egypt had started by the turn of the century but the regional or local press flourished from as far back as 1827. Egypt enjoys a free press. Newspapers are not printed in the Arabic language alone, but have expanded into several languages to aid the spread of facts, figures and ideas from Egypt to different parts of the world. A variety of publications including six daily newspapers, are published. Egypt has radio ties throughout the world, and has established a broadcast network with many 24 hour-a-day stations that reach all levels of modern society. Special attention has been given to local and regional broadcasts, which are aimed at particular communities throughout Egypt. Since television transmission began in 1960, it has been constantly developing. TV has changed from black-and-white to color transmission, and now has two channels so that each one can present particular ideas and programs.

Housing: There are severe crowding problems in the cities. However new, cheap housing projects are helping to solve the problem. Over 96 percent of the population live in 5 percent of the country's area, with 44 percent living in urban areas and the rest living in some 4,000 villages where the populations range from 500–10,000 inhabitants.

Education: Elementary education is available to all children between six and twelve years of age, and is compulsory. Classes are divided into morning and afternoon sessions with the pupils attending one or the other. Schools are co-ed in the elementary and preparatory stages (six to fifteen-year-olds) but are segragated at the secondary stage

Glossary

(fifteen to eighteen-year-olds). Education is free at all levels except in private schools. There are eighteen universities.

Agriculture: Agriculture remains the most important part of Egypt's economy, accounting for nearly 65 percent of exports and employing some 45 percent of the total labor force. Cotton is Egypt's most important export, but sugarcane, onions, potatoes and citrus fruits are also sold extensively to overseas markets. Nearly all cultivation is carried out by peasant farmers whose operations are funded and generally controlled by cooperative organizations. Productivity is usually good. Irrigation and land reclamation schemes have contributed to a small increase in the cultivable area, and is ultimately intended to irrigate nearly 404,200 hectares (one million acres).

distillation   The process of boiling a liquid and collecting its vapor.

felucca   A sailboat commonly used on the Nile River.

geomagnetism   The magnetic field of the earth.

ginning   The process of separating cotton seeds from the raw cotton.

hydroelectricity   Electricity generated by water power.

irrigation   The channelling of water to dry land using artificial canals and ditches.

Islam   The religion of Muslims.

judiciary   Relating to the law.

kohl   A cosmetic powder used to darken the area around the eyes.

Koran   The holy book of Islam.

liquefaction   The process of becoming liquid.

mosque   A Muslim place of worship.

nationalized   Taken over and run by the government.

recession   A period in which the economy of a country goes into a decline.

Index

Abu Simbel 17, 52
Alexandria 14, 18, 28, 33, 41, 54
architecture 34, 35
army 36, 37
Assyut 44
Aswan 6, 16, 26, 27, 54, 55
Aswan Dam 16, 17, 26, 52, 53

Bedouin 35, 42, 43
belly dancing 18, 19

Cairo 6, 10, 18, 20, 31, 50, 51, 56, 57
camels 6, 7, 43
carpets 44, 45
China 10
civil servants 18
climate 41, 49, 58
clothes 35
conservation 13
cotton 14, 15, 34
currency 58

dates 40, 41, 52, 53
Delta, Nile 8, 14, 32

education 53, 58
   schools 22, 26, 28, 29, 40
   universities 20, 21, 29, 34, 39
El Faiyum 22, 30, 31
El Kharga 36, 37, 40, 41, 44
Ethiopia 17

farming 14, 15, 26, 27, 30, 31, 36, 42, 44, 59
felucca 38, 39, 59
fish 13, 33
fishing 32, 33, 39, 42
funerals 53

government 57, 58

housing 58

industry 14, 19, 58
irrigation 14, 39, 59
Israel 12

Jacob Island 10, 11

Koran 21, 23, 59

language 21, 28, 29, 58
Luxor 39, 46, 49, 54

Mariout, Lake 32
marriage 14, 18, 34, 49, 53
media 56, 57, 58
Mediterranean Sea 24, 32
military service 7
mosques 20, 21, 59
Muslims 20, 21, 58

Napoleon 24
Nasser, Lake 17
         President 24
Nile River 10, 16, 32, 33, 38, 47, 54, 55
Nubia 17, 52, 53
Nuweiba 12

oil 8, 9, 42, 54

papyrus 10, 11
Peoples' Assembly 56, 57
pharaohs 47
politics 57, 58
population 23, 58

Red Sea 12, 13, 24
religion 20, 21, 23, 58
Revolution, the 34

scuba diving 12, 13
seismic analysis 9
Sharm El Sheikh 12, 42
ships 25, 27
Sinai 8, 12, 27, 42
sports 12, 13, 26, 27
Sudan 6, 10, 17
Suez Canal 24, 25
   Gulf 8
sugarcane 7, 38, 39

temples 46
Thebes 47
tombs 46, 47
Turkey 19
Tutankhamun 47

War, Six-Day 25
Western Desert 8